Magpie Days

Magpie Days

by

Brenda Sciberras

TURNSTONE PRESS

Turnstone Press
Artspace Building
206-100 Arthur Street
Winnipeg, MB
R3B 1H3 Canada
www.TurnstonePress.com

MIX
Paper from responsible sources
FSC® C016245

Turnstone Press gratefully acknowledges the assistance of the Canada Council for the Arts, the Manitoba Arts Council, the Government of Canada through the Canada Book Fund, and the Province of Manitoba through the Book Publishing Tax Credit and the Book Publisher Marketing Assistance Program.

Printed and bound in Canada by Friesens for Turnstone Press.

Library and Archives Canada Cataloguing in Publication

Sciberras, Brenda, 1958-, author

Magpie days / by Brenda Sciberras.

Poems.

ISBN 978-0-88801-489-4 (pbk.)

I. Title.

PS8637.C597M33 2014 C811'.6 C2014-904423-2

For My Family

In Memory of My Father
Fredric Sciberras (1924–2009)

Contents

Magpie Days

One for sorrow, two for joy,
Three for a girl, four for a boy,
Five for silver, six for gold,
Seven for a secret, never to be told,
Eight's a wish, nine's a kiss,
And ten for a bird you must not miss

Snapshot

Here, I've found that picture
you took of me when I was nine
or ten in my yellow pedal-pushers

standing by the barbed wire fence
next to the cornfield
meekly pointing

at the magpie perched
on a wooden post
amazed that it's

intrigued with me
yet certain to fly away
with the click of your shutter.

Transcona Shops 1958

My father's hands
calloused & gnarled,
fingernails blackened
skin nicked by wheels of steel.

Coal soot collects in his lungs, sweat beads
above his brow, in his ears
a perpetual ring
hum & thunder of the locomotive engine.

When the whistle blows at noon,
he opens his metal lunch box
to peanut butter & jelly sandwiches
wrapped in wax paper, tea & biscuits
shared with pigeons,
feral cats & flutter wings.

Another sunny afternoon
in his pit of darkness
beneath a turbine's shadow
with men who swear & spit rage.
Wop, Polack, Bohunk, & A-rab,
a pecking order of insults.

He waits with the other machinists,
for the four o'clock whistle
& the midway leading
home to catalogue bungalows,
black & white TV
& babies crying.

A New Shade of Blue

We jump into the pickup,
head down five miles of gravel, scavenge
through a sea of other people's junk
until he spots shiny chrome
handlebars & rusty spokes of a rim.

Back home he sands & paints
assembles my new Ford blue bike.
When the paint dries he teaches me to ride,
pushes me down our long driveway
runs behind, lets go only when I begin
to pedal & pedal.

Further down the road I falter, skid
through bulrushes & land in the deep ditch
magpies squawk in disgust,
frogs silence their croak.
I rise wet & scathed.
Haul my bike dripping
onto the gravel
walk it back to the house.

My father smiles, pats my shoulder,
messes my curls calls me his "tough girl."
I laugh & pretend my scraped knee
doesn't hurt & hope my flushed cheeks
don't betray his pride.

Dreaming Ludgarda

We leaf through the Eaton's catalogue
our Saturday afternoon ritual
sit side by side on the flowered sofa & sip tea
imagine that we are rich & can order anything.
You choose a lavender housedress & I pick the white
vanity dresser with the mirror & chair.
We tire of dreaming—
move to the kitchen table to play Fish.
It's the only card game you know.
You let me win & sometimes I let you win,
but we always cheat.

You tell me of your life in the Mediterranean
on the island of Malta, in Sliema
& of the foods you like to eat.
The thought of dining on rabbit & anchovies
horrifies me. You remember as a little girl
you'd wake with the cry of the rooster
& walk barefoot around the rocky island visiting
little villages before the sun set over the citadel.

I am fixed on your dark eyes & bunned hair.
Your words slow as you tell
how you & Grandpa fell in love—
married against both your families' wishes.
With war in the world & between your families
you boarded a boat to Canada
never dreamt you wouldn't return
to your homeland of pillar & stone
or see your family again.

Eternal Youth

My grandmother—wordless
her stubborn Maltese tongue
reluctant to speak this foreign language.

Sixty years in Canada, she
never knew female conversation.
Rode the bus downtown,

spoke to no one but the driver
"I want off at Eaton's & Mitchell-Copp."
She bought a gold-plated music box

with a smooth pearl on top,
a cardigan, burgundy as wine
& a dark-haired walking doll.

Small reminders of finer things she left
behind, perhaps a childhood relived,
as she watched me unwrap them one by one.

She's been gone thirty-five years,
died at eighty-two eternally dark-haired,
my image of her vivid

as my countless grey hairs
& the box of dark-brown colour
waiting on the counter.

Flight of Birds

Confined within the walls
    of this paint peeled
        exterior, I grow sullen.

Insulated from this noxious city
    of cracked concrete
        & bland buildings—

Its bustling arrogance pounding
    at the back door
        I long to open.

I am safe in here, yet restless—
    watch birds outside
        migrate to field & forest.

The world beyond these venetian blinds
    is a pavement parked
        rudeness of lights & noise.

The mayhem of city life
    keeps me tethered here
        robs me of solitude.

I long to become transitory
    grapple with words
        sequester a countryside.

Losing My Marbles

A velvet Crown Royal bag
purple & full of promise.

Loosen the golden silk drawstring
spill the vibrant crystal balls.

Watch the mibs
scramble down

an unworn path of green shag
careen toward endless possibilities

only their glassy weight
carries nothing to obstruct their route.

The glazed click on impact
of ricochet

Alleys & cat's-eye

rolling
rolling
rolling

A kaleidoscope of direction.

Field Guide to the Magpie

You are a garrulous bird
like to hear yourself

yak
yak
yak

thief when you choose to be
steal the sounds of others
your liquid voice often misunderstood.
Should you by chance locate a feeder
stocked with seeds, scatter will
the chickadees.

A nuisance you might say, unloved
in spite of their yearning
for your iridescent tail
the Chinese man down the street
calls you his

bird
of
joy

Monet painted *The Magpie* in winter,
Magnasco tried to tame & teach
you to sing. Bacchus believed you
sacred (did he know you feast on roadkill,
moths, mosquitoes & dung?)

At dawn & dusk you walk a lonely road
a silent pilfer you prefer to be
so, I play *The Thieving Magpie*
Rossini's overture & entice
you to cry

caw

caw

caw

Speed

Homemade dandelion wine
tucked in your purse
with three stolen roll-your-owns.

Your first high school dance, the long-haired
city guy, checking out your tight top,
smooth bend of your jeans.

Music swaying you closer, "Hey Jude"
& "A Horse with No Name."
He calls you "Babe."

In his Chevy. Windows rolled down
stereo blaring, driving into dark
the hue of dash light bares his smile.

He grasps the shift & thrusts into third,
you knew he'd want more than just the ride.
Wind blows your hair wild, gravel kicks out behind.

Hocus Pocus

Found my Ouija board in the basement,
brought it up to the dining room.
Last used over forty years ago,
at a fifteen-year-old's slumber party, girls
giggling, then silence, the floating wooden
heart pointing out letters. Some believed
it was a hoax. Kathy thought it was the devil.
It spelled out who I loved—*K E R R Y*
Had we kissed? *Y E S*
Did I lose my virginity? *N O*
Who did I hate? *M A R L E N E*
Then the candle blew out
& everyone screamed
running for the door. I stayed lit
a match burning my fingertips.

Later, after chips & Dr Pepper
we tried a seance, thought we'd summon
a few dead relatives or friends.
Girls giggling, then silence, the candle
flickering in the dark, our breath
heavy in smoky air. We summoned
Cheryl who died in a car crash on the
May long weekend. Some believed
it was a hoax. Kathy thought it was the devil.
Colleen saw a floating white dress.
Then the candle blew out
& everyone screamed
running for the door. I stayed lit
a match burning my fingertips.

Adolescent Games

Remember the circle game.
Skipping class, hitchhiking
to the park, drinking beer—

Friends laugh & cheer
as two brothers take turns
remove pieces of a girl's clothing,

until she's left standing
in her bra & flowered panties
pleading for her clothes.

In the final round
even these are torn away.
She is lowered to the ground
crying, kicking—praying.

Slut circles the crowd.
Her friends—most laugh—while others
are silent—
fear they'll be next.

The brothers alternate
her ankles & wrists held tight,
the one above her head, looks down

straight into her screaming.
Quietly everyone watches.
No one stops it—

Not even you.

Rite of Passage

Their books are open
they pretend to read

Sigh at mistakes
erase letters raw

Restless fingers
turn & tear pages
from binders

They hush in carrels
not to study but to etch
initials into wood

scratch, I am here

Glass-Blowing

Anger locked inside a shell of a boy.
As years pass, he will be cast
from the same template,
deny any semblance to his parents
emboss a lifetime of overlay.

I try to alter the pattern, transform
or break the mould, quiet his fists
& cool the molten rage within.

In time, we hold hands
his fingers unfold
free the flame
& in that moment of forgetting
I see through his empty iridescent lies.

Wrapped in an intoxicated teardrop,
I turn the melting glass upside down,
shed his inhered yoke.

Birder

He enters the crowded room
with a swaggering strut
thick-soled feet steer him across
the hardwood floor.

> *The black-billed magpie's very long tail*
> *& iridescent colours make it stand out*
> *from the crowd.*

Scarf swaddles the nape of his neck,
head cocked to the right, then left
& forward again.

> *The male bird proves dominance*
> *with an elaborate display by cocking*
> *his head & flashing his eyelids.*

Perched on a stool women gather to him
above chatter & laughter
his wit soars freely.

> *A bird call is made up of various notes*
> *in particular repeating patterns. In many*
> *species only the male sings. His song*
> *attracts a mate & warns other males*
> *to stay out of his territory.*

With this show he's managed
to entice a young lady.
As they migrate from the crowd
I notice how his ass fits his jeans.

The black-billed magpie has metallic
dark blue-green wings & tail.
Large contrasting white markings
on primaries are noticeably visible in flight.

Metamorphic

The landscape of our marriage
   has changed, liquor-logged,
our bed silent as the grave—
   Only the wind kisses my ear.

I take my refuge in poetry
   weave a cocoon of change
emerge into acceptance
   no longer hungover

embrace metaphor
   while you wrap your arms around
Johnnie Walker
   & all the Juicy Fruit in the world
won't mask your denial.

Soon we are enemies
   play hide & seek, not with our children.
Itemize two decades
   divvy assets & diminish heirlooms,
bicker over liabilities.

   Until all that remains are bare walls,
artifacts from another life, a wedding
   photograph framed in tarnished silver
resting against your bottle tombstone.

End-Game

When we play games
like this I don't believe
it's a momentary lapse.

Thought I was your Queen
& you my King, instead
I'm a poisoned Pawn
& you're a fool's mate.

My innocent blunder
let you swindle my trust.
Maybe it's time to forfeit
the match, offer a draw,
find a new opponent.

For this bind bargains
no sacrifice for you,
all your excuses,
have not captured my heart
for any length of ticking time.

Giving to Goodwill

I'll never wear this parka again
it reminds me of my ex
& the time I ran away.

Left the kids tucked in their beds
him seated with his beer
hockey scraping on the screen.

Drove in the snow
to the Safeway parking lot
sat in this parka watched people
walking in & out of the store.

White falling ever so softly
wished I was that snowflake—
any flake, so unique.

Women with bags
full of possibilities
I didn't feel I had.

I'm tired of this old parka
it's off to the Goodwill
aqua a poor choice
for my olive features.
The matching gloves
remind me of that day in January
my friend died—
& I left the hospital absent
one glove.

After her funeral
I returned home to find
the pair neatly folded
together in the glove basket,
as if in prayer—

Still, I'm ready to let go of these old
things, aware that once they're gone
they're gone for good.

Lo Siento

Am I to sit here
brooding over your absence
while you lie on sandcastle
beaches, gazing at hard
bodies that saunter past?

The two of you tour markets
in sandals & khaki shorts,
till you retire for an afternoon
siesta. Later you sample spicy
quesadillas & saucy enchiladas.

Then cool your tongue
with fresh mangos & melons.
At night you walk arm in arm
along festive moonlit streets
pausing at every noisy cabaret

to dance & laugh,
drink margaritas & Corona
with lime till you sing out of tune.

You owe me nothing, *mi amigo.*
Nor I you & yet, if I sent you this poem
which one of us would be sorry?

Housekeeping

In the kitchen where I once stood
she clutches her stainless
steel bowl & wooden spoon,
folding berries & batter.
She's thrown away my measuring cup,
pots & pans, all my utensils.
She's shred the sheets
I once slept on. Fit a new mattress
to her own taste. Stuffed my pillows
into garbage bags, left
at the end of the road.
But my rusty red griddle is still going strong
as she flips pancakes
onto her shiny new plates.

Banff

Here, I soar with birds,
feel the earth
heave & swell beneath me.

I never knew I'd miss you
so much, you say
when I call
from my mountain perch.

You've always been the one
to fly away.
How do I explain
this coexistence of

desire & fear

to fledge—
discover what's beyond?

Still my instinct is strong
luring me back to you.

I imagine I'm a magpie
resting in the cedar outside
our window
recognize your melancholy
ponder the migration home.

Confession

I kneel at the altar
of my Catholic sensibilities—
press the rosary
hard into my fingertips.
Like the host in a priest's hand
when you offer compliments
I receive them humbly.

It's not longing—
I have not been searching,
never wanted you
nor sought you out.
Yet, like a flame in darkness
you flicker into my life—
to haunt my dutiful days.

We share the chalice, savour
words, drain our marriages
sip by sip.
Is this adultery?
I covet your affection.
Our first stolen kiss
a confession.

I will refuse further rendezvous
pray we'll come to our senses
wait for our lives to crumble.

Unsettled

Monday night is the worst,
another dismal week begins—

nothing beyond phone conversation
into the early hours.

You in your Wolseley apartment
me uncertain in the quiet country,

chilled even beneath the covers.
I toss & turn the restless hours—

dream of your squeaky single bed
unravel my twisted-sheet nights.

Finally, Friday
Driving through a blizzard

I reach your crowded city street
white-knuckled.

An unfamiliar bed holds us both.
The newness of your skin & bone—

you feel it too. The curve
of my pelvis different from hers.

When I go, separation leaves
me unsettled, blurs my vision

as wipers sweep
wet snow from my windshield.

leaving—
is harder, storm or not.

Bella Vista

We walk arm in arm under a canopy of elms,
down Wolseley to Maryland the first snow
crunches beneath our feet.

Enter the Bella Vista, the aroma of garlic
like a blanket, as we're ushered without hesitation
to our usual table along the banister.

The ambiance of this factitious place
makes us want to travel across the sea,
its Tuscan murals & candelabras
each missing one light.

Not the usual crowd of singles
at the bar, or couples at tables,
no gamblers behind the curtain.

Tonight is different; it's All Saints' Day,
only a few faces familiar, reflected
in the mirrored wall. Peter Jordan's gang

laughs over pitchers of beer,
Patrick O'Connell, guitar in hand,
waits to serenade us with the blues.

The band sings "Amazing Grace"
& "Let the Circle Be Unbroken" summons
memories, of an earlier time, of pews & penance.

We skip the calamari,
down our red wine
& slip back into cold night air.

The Art of Gardening

Convince me
We should plant a garden together.
Peel away sod, scatter rocks,
break apart clumps of soil, thrash out
poplar roots exposing rich earth.

Convince me
Our garden variety will be more succulent.
Melon holding its vine, sugar peas
cradled in pods, sweet corn cloaked
in silk waiting to be shucked.

Convince me
We should get down on our knees,
surrounded by eager weeds & pull the ugliness
in the midst of such beauty.
Every breath choked by couch grass & thistle,
prune back excess foliage, clear borders.

Convince me
Our bed of stems & blossoms swaying
in a patch of brilliant colour can survive?
Can we immerse our hands
in damp soil & sow what we intend?

Convince me,
again.

Accumulation

His ex calls for trivial reasons,
a flurry of excuses, drifting
into the past.
He remains composed
holds his tongue
calm for the sake of his children.
I forecast a meltdown
if this pattern persists.

Outside another storm looms
on this Christmas Eve—
snow swirls under street lights,
wind sings at our door.
I hope it ends soon.
Never-ending flakes, subtle
yet, in accumulation
the whiteout leaves us all lost.

Yin & Yang

I flick the furnace fan off—
savour silence.
You flick it back on
insist it blocks outside noise—
traffic, sirens, barking dogs
& children—

a hum of havoc, I say.
Noise piggybacking noise.

When I finally fall,
white drifts into my sleep
I'm sucked into the whirling vortex
of Kachina Woman.

Later in a dream, next to you
in the Shelby, top rolled down
Arizona wind riding
through my tangled hair
her roar opens my eyes
to the sound of your snore
while my still vibrating body
tunes the bells
of another Sunday morning.

August

We move like zombies on the beach
sift sand, broken shells
& pebbles for washed up storm glass.

Misshapen fragments cobalt
blue, emerald green & frost
white an expanding spectrum.

Treasure to be stowed away
as rare as the remaining heat–
filled days of August.

The haze & high
humidity of mid-afternoon
labours our breath languid

our bodies slumped in squat chairs
gulls & boats sail in the distance
a mantra of waves laps our shoreline

steals our concentration. In time
heat propels our sunscreen-slathered
bodies into the lake

we emerge with vigour
continue to hunt for more glass
in the shimmer of a dying summer.

Canyon Daze

Winnipeg snow & slush
left behind, we reach the Grand
Canyon. Chasm of time,
step back, breathless
before the scar of preservation
so vast & deep—

We hike the rim
of sublime grandeur,
where eagles & wildcats
defy depths
a sudden gust blows
thought into another realm—

I envision thousands
of souls—hikers & burros
navigating the switchback.
The folded contours
of my body cling
to the rail, petrified
as stone.

Desert Relief

Reckless we leave
the top down
allow black leather
seats to absorb the sting
of midday rays

While we walk
through prickly pear
& brittlebush
our ankles
scratched raw.

Along the scorched trail
a diamondback
rattles at our sandalled feet
& heat blisters
bare shoulders.

We find momentary relief
in the shade
of a giant saguaro
cactus its arms held up
wide to open blue sky.

Burrowing owl hoots
within, golden eagle
screeches above until
we ascend to a rocky ridge
where the horizon
paints away our white
northern winters.

100 Minutes with an Author

We scavenge like magpies,
scribble each uttered word
every sacred syl-la-ble an answer
the antidote,
to another rejection.

She feeds us confidence,
slakes our thirst for validation
what works for her will work for us.

We peck & peck, try to crack the code,
a pathetic flock,
hanging on every word, literally.
Tell me the music you listen to
when you write (so I can listen too).

I wander home feathered in faith
clutch pen to write a poem
littered with shiny words
like *flutter & peel,*
call them my own.

Poets Write Poetry

fill pages enough for a book
so people will read them
late into the night
eyelids heavy & falling.
Poets write poetry
bite their fingernails
to the quick while making up metaphors
so granddaughters & grandsons
can turn pages with their thumbs
sound words out loud
to their dads & mums.
Poets write poetry
so people can say
what do you write
& what's it about?
Poets write poetry
so librarians can shelve books
readers might memorize
to recite the rhythm of their lives.
Poets write poetry to remember
their youth, where they've been
question where they're going.

Believer

I feel like I'm at an old-time sideshow
a levitation demonstration
from the turn of the century.
Gathered in this candlelit
loft of a country machine shed,
we fix our watches, fidget,
& fuss as nervous conversation
drifts around the room.
I analyze shadows
lurking behind each woman.
Latecomers are seated as sweet grass
smolders in the circle's centre.
I'm not sure who our *medium* will summon
or why they'll come.
We rise & clasp hands,
say a prayer of protection & gratitude
to the Gods & Spirits who may manifest.
We become *sitters* & turn silent.
She closes her eyes, slowly
rocks back & forth.
When she is ready & receptive,
occupied with the spirit of the dead
she waves her hand in my direction
Asks: *do you know someone named Linda?*
& I do.
Speaks of boundaries I need to break,
how rules & regrets race through my realm.
Says: *you're a bit of a saint,*
you sometimes give too much.

The skeptic in me thinks yes,
I've just given a stranger twenty bucks
to tell me what I already know.

Fledgling

Her tenacious curiosity
finds an electrical socket
blackens her delicate fingertips.

At seven, her teacher calls to say—
she's stolen Fruit Roll-Ups
from a classmate's backpack.

My time-out sanctions create
a cackling crescendo:
I hate you, I want a new mom—
from behind her bedroom door.

Each passing year—
I gather new transgressions
fumble in the darkness
of motherhood

grapple with aversion
to adolescent tattoos & piercings
F-bombs flung
at my *it's for your own good!*

When she sneaks out to a forbidden party
I take her door from its hinges—
its return a Christmas present,
the only item on her wish list.

At sixteen the phone rings
an hour past curfew—
she's rolled her '79 Mustang in the ditch.

I arrive to headlights
beaming through the night sky
upside-down engine still running
her first car never even makes it
home from the lot—

I spare scolding overlook the heap
of crumpled metal feel the heat of her
life flashing before my tear-filled eyes.

Remains

We search for her
collar & tags among
the black fur, shattered skull
& open belly.

My young daughter
holds the box
for the blood
& bones.

While I slide the shovel
beneath what remains
sprawled
on the open highway.

I place our dog
& shovel in the trunk,
leave behind a smear
of crimson.

We drive through the countryside
in silence.
In a field I dig a hole
lower her

fill this grave
waiting for its body
any body
flesh is flesh.

In the cold
mourning
our eyes meet
as we shovel.

Freezer Burn

i have relatives who kept
their dead dog Dixie
in the deep-freeze
wondered if they wrapped her
in brown freezer paper
bagged her
or just tossed her in
next to the chickens & ground beef

the dog they claimed died
after the ground froze
& that they would give her a proper burial
after the spring thaw

it was a long bitter cold winter
i've never seen Dixie's grave
or eaten at their table since.

Journey

i went on a journey—
rode on a black horse along

crisp blue edges of a sunny brook
crossed the clear water & watched

a field flame with fire—
remembering *the camera my mother gave me*

boundaries blurred—
i tried to snap a photograph,

but my horse became *too hot to handle*
& i dropped hard to the ground below.

upon wakening i heard the echo
of my childhood brother calling me

crybaby! whenever i stumble—
two or three things i know for sure

i am tenacious even without
my *map to the door of no return*

i act as any sure *soldier* would
& consult the book of Jessica.

as i read of another woman's life
echoes of my grandmother's suffering—

what does a woman want?

what do I want?

On Gozo

Citrus groves call out
to me, tangled gardens

of gold, seek to keep me
captive much like Odysseus

who stayed seven years.
I envision him picking

lemons from that tree,
walking the path

along this stone fence
topped with twisted vines,

running his fingers over its damp
& ancient rock.

Now, I come to stand above towering
cliffs of his Calypso's Cave

where olive branches weave
their way down to the morning

valley haze & red sands
of Ramla Bay.

When I vanish from this glimmering
fragrance-soaked island

just as he did, will the wind-weathered faces
    & stone temples tug as hard

upon my Homeric soul?

Lunar Cycle

Forgotten are those nebulous nights
   sweat beading between my breasts,
laughter easy off my tongue.

But now, in this season of decay
   as gravity robs me of youth,
once firm, now fleshy

& like a sudden storm,
   a burst of rain, I too rest
on the threshold of tears.

I know the cycle comes to an end—
   that warm red flow
where pain & pleasure gather.

Just as the evening primrose unfurls,
   its bloom fades, its sweet
perfume subsides in the midday sun.

Still, in spite of this cessation
   under a waning moon, wilted
leaves falling to the dry ground,

I know it's not the end of me, as leaf lustre
   surrenders to withering branches
& snow descends on the barren prairie—

I grow luminous.

Casbah

I have joined a caravan of women
eastern music luring me closer
to my body's
swaying rhythm.

doum doum teca tec
          doum doum teca
                    tec

dark eyes dart above sheer silk
arms snake & shoulders entice,
hips rotate mystery
pewter coins jingle
on a chiffon sash,
bangles & bracelets
sing of seduction.

doum doum teca tec
          doum doum teca
                    tec

I glide across the stage floor
bare feet flash iridescent nails.
Willow body twists & winds
zills chime & hands sculpt desire
in casbah spectators
who watch my sequined
shimmy dance a circle.

I am priestess, I am goddess.

doum doum teca tec
doum doum teca
tec

Momentum

I set out for the hoodoos
  over shale & spruce
venture alone through inclines & recesses
  for a broader view.

Hit my stride after the first river bend
  becoming sure-footed I move
with ease over tangled roots that snake
  across the winding path.

The higher I climb the clearer it becomes—
  turning back is not an option.

I pause in an alcove above the treetops
  here time stands still,
subsists within my breath.

These mountains stand witness—
  awaken my soul.

Snow begins to fall, heavy & wet on my lashes.
  The forest grows surreal
fir trees laden with white
  whisper *this* way.

Casting Off

Strands unravelling,
fraying the familiar
fabric, the pattern
altered by events,
or knots.
I didn't mean
to drop a stitch, not notice
until it was too late to recover.
Stitch by stitch, smaller & smaller
the pattern became. Casting
off was the hardest part. I had never
cast off before this, didn't have
instructions on how to end.
A family, scatter children,
begin again, again as a spent
woman. No longer a flushed firm
adolescent in love with love,
learning to cast on, arrange cupboards,
fold laundry, add
spice, create a kingdom,
fortress of safety,
a family album. Eventually
set a table for five,
decrease stitches
four, three,
two, then one.
knit one,
purl two,
leave enough yarn,
yarn to cast
off.

Thieving Magpie

You gather all that shines
bright—within her
as we watch her fade
before our eyes.

You begin—
with her breast
& she's left with one.
Then her copper locks
fall prey & pray she does—
believes she's chased you off.

But, you're a trickster—
sneak into her skull, peck away
at her spine, steal her legs—
a wheelchair, her cage.

In the end—
you rob us—of her.

Oh, lone magpie—
where will you hide
her glittering soul?

Carousel

You listen
for your name
its echo
within
white waiting walls

You've entered this
revolving door before
still
the fear of leaving
altered
misshapen
frames every thought

It seems there's always
a new lump
larger
than the last

The doctor's constant chatter
a gracious attempt
to quiet
frayed nerves
you grasp
nothing

When the needle
pierces
tender skin
cradling your areola
you focus
on a painting

Three little girls
riding a carousel
ponytails flying
in a cirrus sky
faces smiling

Look ahead

Absence

I imagine you standing naked
before the mirror—ache to touch
each round protuberance
flesh of womanhood
cut away to live—

It wasn't enough to lose
your breasts.

Sometimes in the dark of night
in the act of love,
at the moment of touch
caress & kiss
arousal—

I think of you—
breasts replaced by scars
running deep into a hollow
never to heal.

Still Waiting

I've come for my final visit,
yet feel like I'm intruding
lay next to her body
curled like a leaf wilted at the end
of a hot day.

I look into her once beautiful face
now swollen from drugs, her pale
hand in mine & for a moment
gather myself
so she won't see my tears.

Her pain—morphine suspended
mine above the breastbone.
Still, her failing heart pumps
through its translucent shell,
her laboured breath
will soon betray.

Perhaps, I should have
said more. But, I'd read somewhere
that the dying don't like chatter.
It was enough to hold their hand,
just to be there—still

Why didn't I tell her
that she'd been the loveliest of friends?
That I will always think
of her in this month of May
when spring flowers bloom

or on her September birthday
when the golden leaves
let go—& fall
back to earth.

Sea Swell

The cancer's wretched tenacity
  has left her lurching.

Its treatment prolongs
  her drowning.

Grabbing the edge of death
  jerked back

like a carp on a fisher-
  man's line, the heave-ho

of the fight. Close enough
  to the light to be reborn.

The greenscape outside the window
  pane rocks & sways.

Second-Hand

I read you
like a well-worn book.
Your poetic dog-eared pages
broken spine &
cancer-ridden corners.
An intricate journey
of life leaking
from flesh & bone,
raw with pain.
The fruits of all metaphors
ferment with disease,
wither.
Readers devour
my second-hand imagery
of tubes, bags,
bruises & meds.
They all want to know
what the book's about?
How long? How does it end?
Christ, I don't know
I haven't finished yet.
If only I could
mend your broken
spine, tape your verso, bring
you back into circulation
as any good librarian should.

Remembrance

November
sadness propels you to paint poppies
in watercolour.
A year has passed,
in revelation & regret
leaving
your soul weary with sorrow.

With the first snow
his chores left undone—
winter tires, Christmas lights
& weatherstripping.
His guitar in the corner
his picture on the wall,
the kangaroo-skin hat he wore
to Folk Fest abandoned to a hook.

He is nowhere, yet everywhere,
your love—frozen in place.
The silence too intense
the house empty, yet still full.
There are days you
stay warm in your bed
feel his breath closest there.

It's like walking in the dark
can't see what lies ahead
afraid of each solitary step.

Wine & chocolate futile comfort
your solace—scripture.
Yet, autumn after autumn
fallen leaf after fallen leaf
the tears will still come.

The Canadian Shield

I dream you & I are riding on a train—
  splendour of prairie flax blue
& golden canola—
  sway past the window.

Soon, forests flicker sunlight & shade
  pines tower above rock risen
from Precambrian ground.
  In the dream the train stops

in the middle of nowhere—
  to let us walk up
the mossy slope & pick wild blueberries.
  We eat more than we pail

laugh more than we speak
  & you are not sick.
We board & continue our journey
  head no place in particular.

Time on our side—
  & you as strong
 as the bedrock
   beneath the rails.

Vision

The pelican sails silently
inches above the waves far from
the leafy shoreline of birch & poplar.

A sudden soar, almost heavenly
until her shadow moves
across my blank page.

Her orange bill & pouch,
wings stretched seven feet,
black-edged jagged feathers oily

ready for water.
I'm amazed at what I can see
with my new eyeglasses.

Can she see
me down here watching
her graceful matinee?

The pelican's slow ascent
from my sight
spurs me, writing.

Magpie Days

The magpie can sit
on your bare back & peck—
until your bones sparkle
& sing with wind.

You know you've given
it a good run. Tasted wild
grass & sweet alfalfa grazed—
through many a day's yellow sun.

Now the bell stops ringing
around your neck, no more
boundaries, no more stalls—
skies are clear & blue.

Fidel

Picture him ageless,
at the kitchen table
lifting a candle from yet another
birthday cake set before him.
Any other time he would be
building assembling fixing
using those work-battered hands
for something less indulgent.

I always took his name for granted
until *Fidel* appeared on the nameplate
above his hospital bed
his body constantly cold,
even tucked beneath my red blanket.
His beard in one last stage
of growth & grey
thick glasses obscuring
the true clarity of his vision.

He tells me the nuns, who taught him,
thought his name too foreign,
changed it to *Fredric*.
In these final days words come easy,
our memories like a shutter flickering.
I thought there'd always be another cake,
another photo to frame.

Old Birds

The first warm day
& I watch
birds fly back & forth
twigs & branches
in their curved beaks.
They're building a nest
in the eaves beyond
my second-floor window.

From the seniors home across the lane
old men & women emerge
shuffle to the end of the sidewalk
coax their frail bodies,
inch by inch. Walkers gripped
tightly in their white-knuckled fists
each small step closer
to where the concrete ends.

It's a precious patch of dry pavement
that brings them close enough to notice
the bird's toil under my eaves.
Their wrinkled faces grin in the sun,
then a careful turn & gradual migration
back from where they began
the odd cackle when two pass
as the birds flutter back & forth.

Semi-Private

Beyond the doorway
lights flicker
shadows pass
plastic trays on rolling carts
clatter a tune
smells marry smells
monitors blink & beep
whispers behind the partition
elevator doors
open & close
close & open
while I wait
listen
as my father's lungs
rattle to the rhythm.

Lucky Man

My father says it's a lucky man
who can down a cold glass of water—

as I hand him a white Styrofoam cup
with a single chip of ice

watch as he slides it around on his tongue
now wet & alive.

We don't talk of when he could swallow
before the fall & the tube to his stomach.

He says he needs to shed
his hospital-blue pyjamas

escape his brutal bed
shuffle through the revolving door—

drive back to his garden
next to the highway

carry pails of glistening rainwater
to ladle over his parched bedding plants.

He says, *they must be thirsty.*

Etching

Sitting up in his hospital bed
arms outstretched
my father summons us
to *gather around,*
shakes one chastening finger
& lovingly commands
don't cry for me.
But we will.

Later alone in the dim of night
he traces my face
runs his fingers through my curls
outlines my features as though to etch
them deep into his memory.

We both know our time
is brief.
Silence our comfort.
I take his work-worn hand
use my finger
trace each line
a gentle sketch.

Foreshadow

My daughters & I sit cross-legged
scatter photographs across
the hardwood floor
shear unnecessary overlap,
paste up memories
for my father's funeral.

Decades of dinner table
birthday cakes. A blur
of candles & presents,
dad sipping his tea—
mum cutting a too-big piece.

Strangely absent—
prairie sky, the seasons he tended—
his tractor & truck.

In retrospect, he spent more time
outside than in & yet,
so many pictures without horizons—
eighty-five years spread out
on a poster board
somehow not enough—

In the end, we drape his denim jacket
& hat around the easel,
his beat-up boots below—
at the centre a picture—
yesterday's sun leaving
his now fallow garden.

Family Tree

I see it now
out in the yard
maple branches reaching—

planted as windbreak decades ago.
My parents never believed
it would grow so high.

So strong, its thick limbs
can swing a grandchild
an enticement to climb

higher follow their imaginations.
I envision when I've grown old
their children too will

collect its fallen leaves
press them between pages
admire what they've made.

Train of Thought

Words float
  around the dinner table,

plates steaming with spaghetti
  your remembered voice—
I could eat this every day.

The apparition of your hands
  gesturing to yet another rail yard story—

I can't part with your ragged grey cardigan
  or this duct-taped radio—
things—keep you here.

You always said *ghosts are hogwash,*
  yet you haunt me.

A train rumbles out back
  reignites my grief—
each whistle blast another question—

hear your response race past
  echoing an absence I cannot silence.

The Seasons of You

In the heat of summer,
your straw cowboy hat
& denim jacket, gone
from the bee-blooming garden.

Fall, the potatoes not dug,
onions not laid out
to dry & the beans
not shelled.

Now, winter blows drifts
down the driveway, piles
snow at the back door,
you are frozen in memory.

And when spring arrives
the sowing of seeds
will begin & our grief
will flourish.

Notes

"One for sorrow": The old children's nursery rhyme was adapted and used as the theme song for *Magpie,* a British children's television series that ran from 1968-1980 (Wikipedia).

"A New Shade of Blue"*:* Ford blue—Made by the Ford Motor Company, this touch-up paint or engine enamel was sold in a spray can and purchased from Princess Auto.

"Birder": The italicized information was taken from the website http://www.allaboutbirds.org/guide/Black-billed_Magpie/life history.

"*Lo Siento*": is Spanish for I am sorry.

"Yin & Yang" Shelby—The Shelby GT-H 2007 convertible is a high performance variant of the Ford Mustang. The fortieth anniversary gold-on-black limited edition is only available at Hertz Rent-a-Car. Kachina Woman—A funnel-shaped rock formation on the Boynton Canyon Trail in Sedona, Arizona. In Hopi legend, Kachina Woman is a guardian and divine protector. She is the only male/female energy vortex that exists in the Southwest, as others are either male or female energy. This vortex is said to strengthen the masculine/feminine or yin/yang balance.

"100 Minutes with an Author" is for Charlene Diehl.

"Fledgling" is for my girls: Rheanna, Jessica, & Alyssa.

"Remains" is for Rheanna.

"Journey": A version of this poem was written during a class at University of Manitoba taught by Dr. Roewan Crowe titled *Writing Women's Lives.* The italicized words are titles of feminist books or articles from the course.

"On Gozo": Gozo—Smaller sister island to Malta. Calypso's Cave—Tradition has it that Gozo is Homer's Ogygia, the island where the nymph Calypso held the Greek hero Odysseus captive for seven years.

"Thieving Magpie," "Still Waiting," and "Second-Hand" are in memory of Linda Elke-Faris.

"Absence" and "The Canadian Shield" are in memory of Melanie Catellier.

"Remembrance" is for Shannon Schultz.

Acknowledgements

To the editors of the following publications in which some of these poems have appeared in an earlier form & some under different titles: *Room of One's Own*, *CV2*, *Rhubarb*, *The Literary Review of Canada*, and the anthology *A/Cross Sections: New Manitoba Writing*.

Sincere thanks to Jamis Paulson, Sharon Caseburg, Sara Harms, Dennis Cooley, & the folks at Turnstone Press for agreeing to publish my first book with such excitement & confidence. I am truly grateful.

To my diligent editor Clarise Foster, who has the keen eye & patience of a magpie. To Lori Cayer who assisted me in editing an earlier draft of the manuscript. To The Manitoba Writers' Guild Sheldon Oberman Mentorship Program & Chandra Mayor who mentored me through earlier versions of some of the poems in the book.

To the Manitoba Arts Council, the Winnipeg Arts Council, & The Banff Centre for the financial assistance that allowed me to write this book. Thank you.

To Sue Goyette ("The Poem Starts Here") & Phil Hall, two of the finest mentors I could have asked for, & the Sage Hill Writing Experience group (2003), where it all really began.

To The Banff Centre Wired Writing Studio faculty & fellow writers (2009) for the inspiration.

To Luann Hiebert, Gerry Wolfram, & Jim Anderson, for camaraderie & critiquing. To my past writers' groups who have lent a hand in the evolution of this book.

To my mom Stella & brother Lloyd for their interest & support throughout the years.

To my three "Little Women," Rheanna Olson, Jessica Hale, & Alyssa Scott, who have all of their lives graciously endured their mother's private time spent studying, reading, & writing. You are truly loved.

To my long-time friends Lorraine McCormick, Kathy Kolisnyk & Sandy Stechisen for lending an ear, offering a shoulder, or just plain asking.

To my family, extended family, friends & colleagues who attend my readings & encourage my writing endeavours. Thank you.

Always to my husband David Elias, last, but certainly not least, for his advice, editing & unwavering support. Much love & gratitude.